ASTOR PIAZZOLLA

CONTENTS

About Astor Piazzolla

Astor Piazzolla was the foremost composer and ambassador of tango music, who carried the signature sound of Argentina to clubs and concert halls around the world. By blending tango with elements of classical music and jazz, Piazzolla sometimes drew fire from tango traditionalists in his native country, even as he won a broad new audience for his bold, uncompromising style.

From the beginning, Piazzolla's music was strongly influenced by his experiences living and studying abroad. He was born in 1921 in Mar del Plata, on the coast south of Buenos Aires, but lived in New York City from 1924 to 1937. In New York the young Piazzolla tuned into the vibrant jazz scene and leading composers, arrangers, and bandleaders such as Duke Ellington and Cab Calloway. At age 12, Piazzolla received his first bandoneon, a large and complex type of button accordion that is the principal voice of tango, and began playing music from the classical repertoire. Soon after his family returned to Argentina in 1937, Piazzolla joined the popular tango orchestra of Anibal Troilo and—while still a teenager—established himself as a talented bandoneon player and arranger.

In Argentina, Piazzolla continued to study classical music, too, with the composer Alberto Ginastera and others. In 1954, Piazzolla's composition "Buenos Aires" (for symphony orchestra with bandoneon) won him a scholarship to study in Paris with influential teacher Nadia Boulanger, who was mentor to Aaron Copland, Virgil Thomson, and many other composers. At the time, Piazzolla was composing in the European classical style, yet Boulanger encouraged him to find his own voice by tapping into his passion for tango. Back in Argentina in the late 1950s, Piazzolla did just that, laying the groundwork for what become known as tango nuevo—new tango.

In 1960 he formed his seminal group Quinteto Tango Nuevo, featuring bandoneon alongside violin, guitar, piano, and bass in an ensemble style intended for the concert stage rather than dance hall, tango's traditional venue. In the ensuing years Piazzolla's music increasingly used dissonance, metrical shifts, counterpoint, and other techniques inspired by modern classical composition and jazz orchestras. In Argentina, where tango is a source of national pride and identity, some tango purists were incensed by these radical departures from tradition, and in the late 1960s even Argentina's military government criticized Piazzolla for being too avant-garde. Audiences in the United States and Europe, however, responded enthusiastically to Piazzolla's innovations, and eventually the controversies in Argentina faded as Piazzolla's artistic accomplishments became clear.

Piazzolla relocated to Europe in the mid-1970s and performed worldwide for the next decade while composing a wide range of music, from concertos to film and theater scores. He returned to Buenos Aires in 1985, where he remained until his death in 1992, at the age of 71.

Piazzolla left behind a huge body of music—more than 750 works—and classic recordings such as *Adiós Nonino* and *Tango: Zero Hour*, as well as collaborations with artists as diverse as poet/author Jorge Luis Borges (*El Tango*), jazz vibraphonist Gary Burton (*The New Tango*), and the Kronos Quartet (*Five Tango Sensations*). In 1986, Piazzolla's music was featured in the Broadway hit *Tango Argentino*. In the years since Piazzolla's death, a broad range of artists have continued to interpret and record his music, from guitarist David Tanenbaum (*El Porteño*) to cellist Yo-Yo Ma (*Soul of the Tango*). In 2001 Amadeus Press published *Astor Piazzolla: A Memoir*, the remarkable life story (as told to journalist Natalio Gorin) of one of the 20th century's true musical iconoclasts.

6

ADIOS NONINO

By YVES PAUL MARTIAL PUECH
and ASTOR PIAZZOLLA

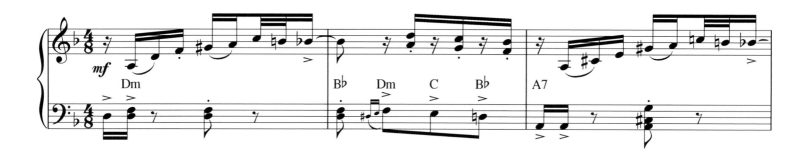

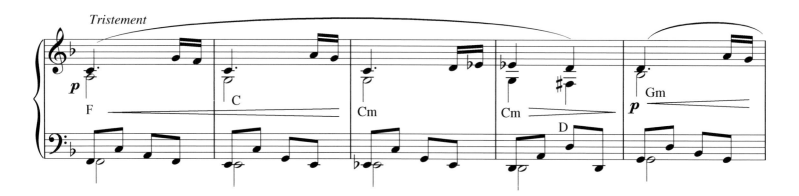

BUENOS AIRES HORA CERO

By ASTOR PIAZZOLLA

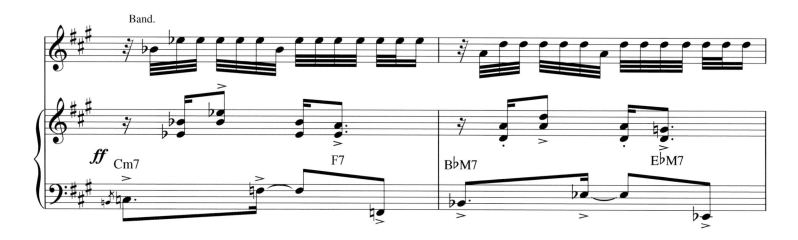

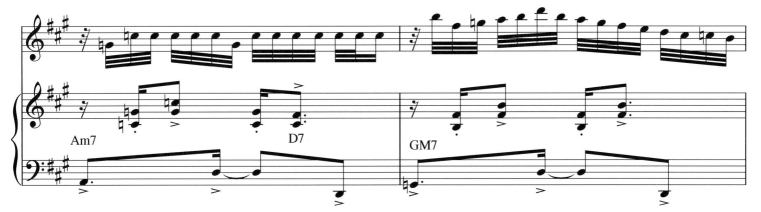

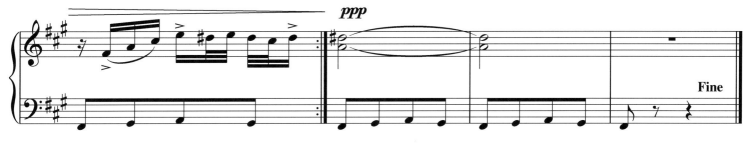

CALAMBRE

By ASTOR PIAZZOLLA

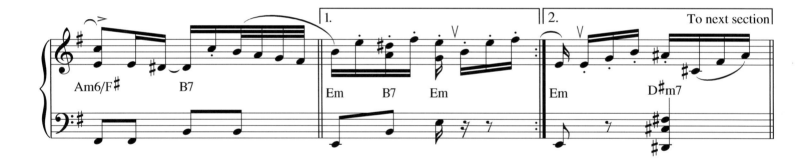

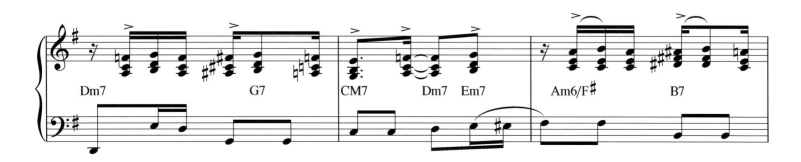

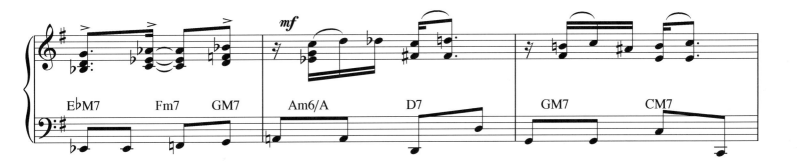

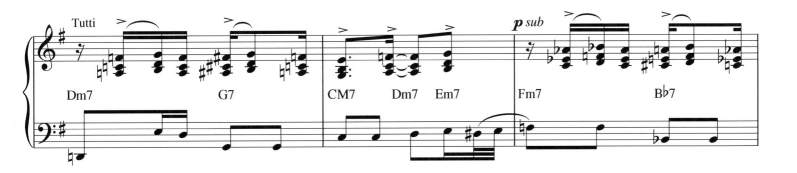

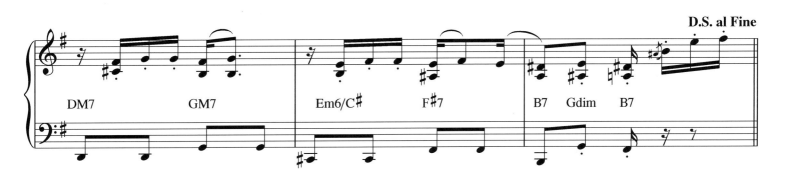

DECARISIMO

By ASTOR PIAZZOLLA

Tango Energico

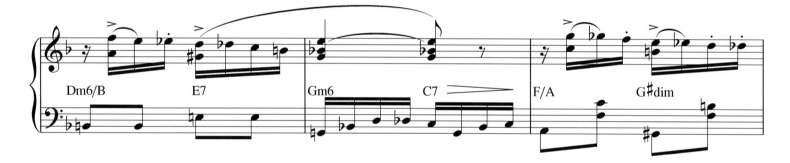

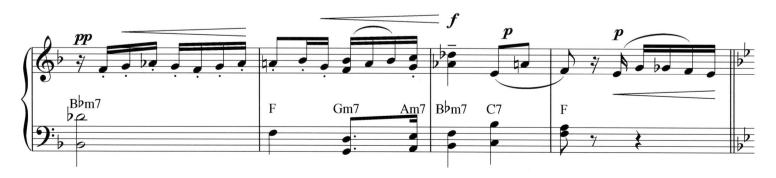

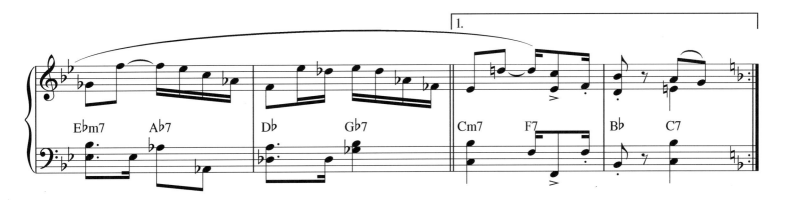

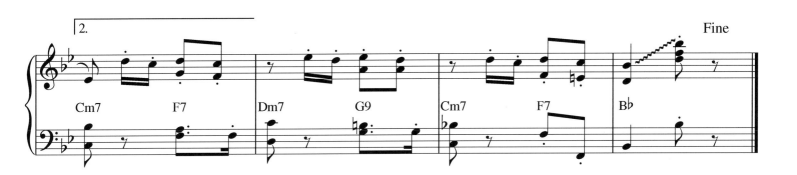

DERNIER LAMENTO

Piano (Synthé) - Chant - Bandonéon (Accordéon) - Violon

By ROGER AUGUSTE, CHARLES DESBOIS,
ALBERT ABRAHAM, BEN SOUSSAN
and ASTOR PIAZZOLLA

- nir?   Dans   le jour qui se meurt   En vain, j'en ai peur,   J'at -
- rais.   Mais   le jour ap - pa - raît   Sans chang - er ma vie,   Tant

- tends!   J'at - tends, car c'est fou com - me je t'ai - me!   J'at - tends pour mieux me trom - per moi -

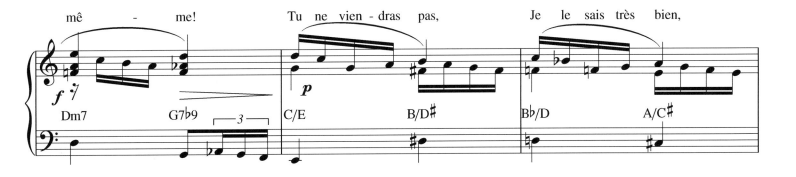

mê - me!   Tu ne vien - dras pas,   Je le sais très bien,

Mais je vis pour ça, je n'y peux rien!   **D.S. al Coda**   CODA   pis!

Espero porque te quiero tanto
Locamente espero sin creerlo
Tu no volveras
Y no volveras
Y lo se muy bien
Pero vivo para eso... si!

1. Estoy como la flor
Como una flor marchita
Que grita su lamentación
Porque se muera el dia
Mucho te quiero a ti
Y tu lo sabes bien
Piedad vuelva hacerme feliz
Y nunca mas a tormentar
Mi pobre corazón
Que te espera con fervor.

2. Viviendo sin tu amor
Sin saber donde estas
Suspiro con desesperación
Cantando el ruego adios, Dios !...
Ay ! si tu corazón
Oyera mi cantar
Seguro te perdonare
Mi alma herido de dolor
Cansado de sufrir
Sin remedio a mi pasión.

EL MUNDO DE LOS DOS

By ALBINO ALBERTO GOMEZ
and ASTOR PIAZZOLLA

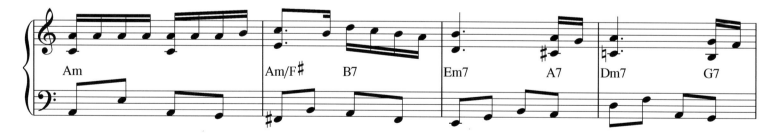

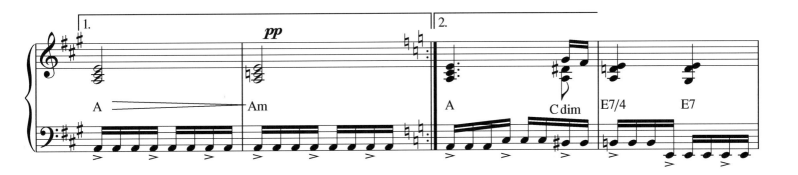

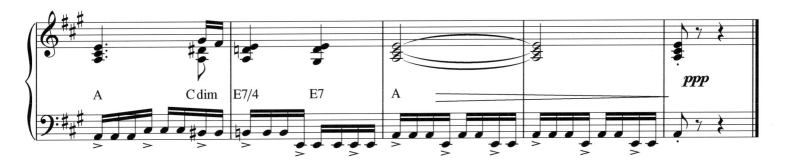

EXTASIS

Piano (Synthé) - Chant - Bandonéon (Accordéon) - Violon

By ASTOR PIAZZOLLA

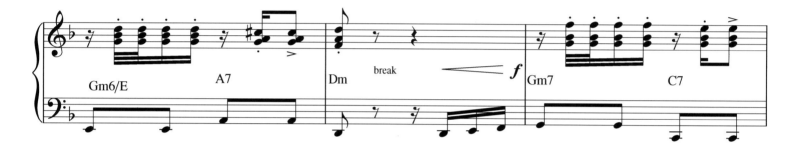

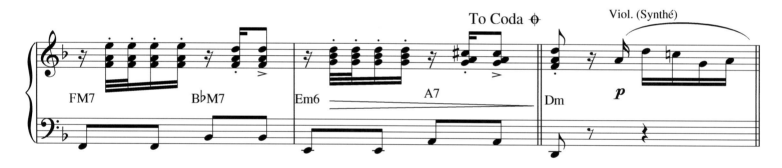

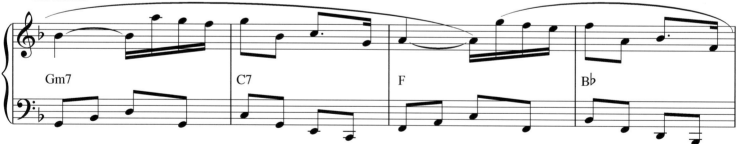

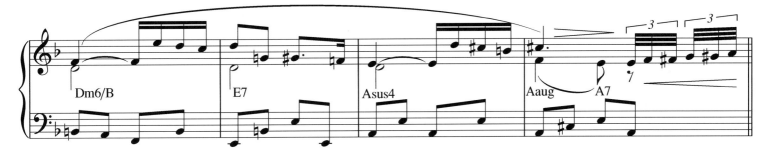

D.S. al Coda

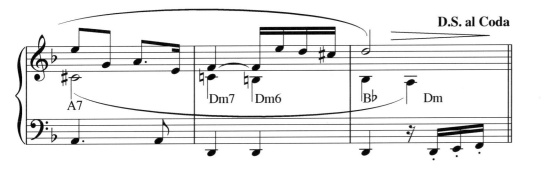

Coda

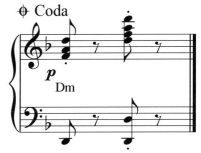

FIÈVRE
(Fiebre de tango)

By ALBERT ABRAHAM, BEN SOUSSAN
and ALBERT NOEL de MARIGNY ENGEURRAND

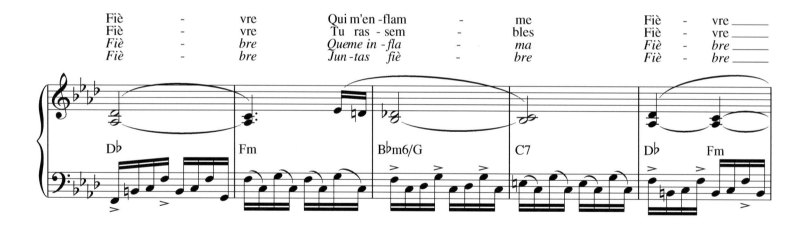

Fiè - vre   Qui m'en -flam - me   Fiè - vre _____
Fiè - vre   Tu ras - sem - bles   Fiè - vre _____
Fiè - bre   Queme in -fla - ma   Fiè - bre _____
Fiè - bre   Jun -tas   fiè - bre   Fiè - bre _____

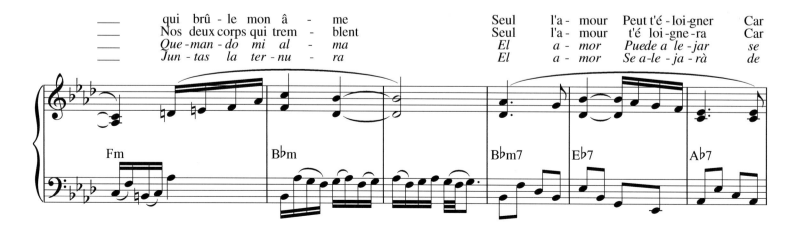

_____ qui brû - le mon â - me   Seul   l'a - mour   Peut t'é -loi-gner   Car
_____ Nos deux corps qui trem - blent   Seul   l'a - mour   t'é loi-gne-ra   Car
_____ *Que-man -do mi al - ma   El   a - mor   Puede a le -jar   se*
_____ *Jun -tas   la ter-nu - ra   El   a - mor   Se a-le - ja - rà   de*

FRACANAPA

PIANO - BANDONÉON (Accordéon) - VIOLON (Synthé) - BASSE

By ASTOR PIAZZOLLA

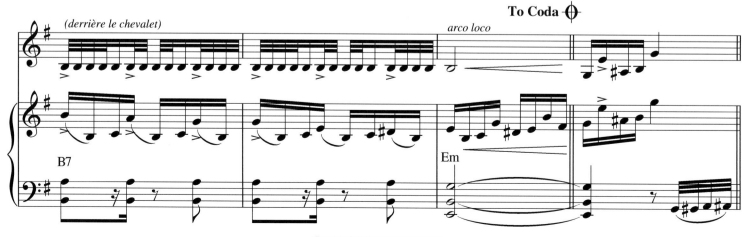

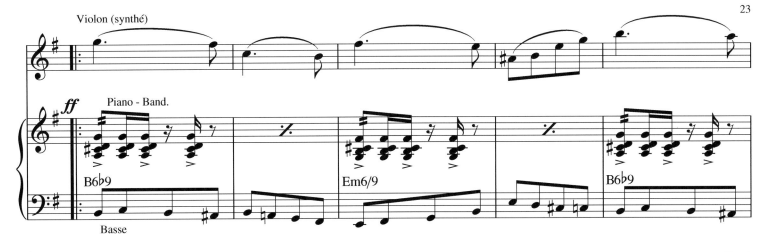

GREENWICH

By ALBERT ABRAHAM, BEN SOUSSAN,
ANDRE PSIETO and ASTOR PIAZZOLLA

GULINAY

By ASTOR PIAZZOLLA

Melancolicamente

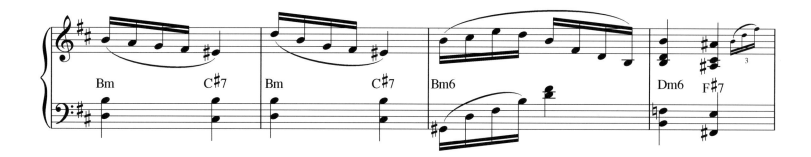

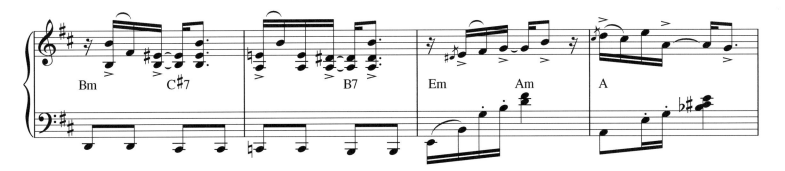

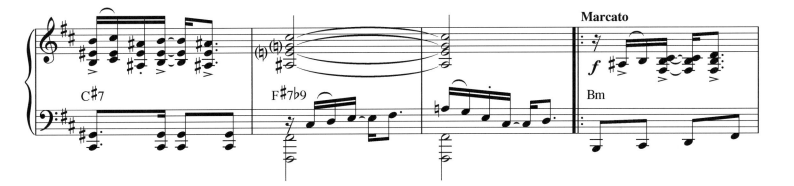

D.C. al Coda

CODA

IMÁGINES 676

PIANO - BANDONÉON (Accordéon) - VIOLON (Synthé) - BASSE

By ASTOR PIAZZOLLA

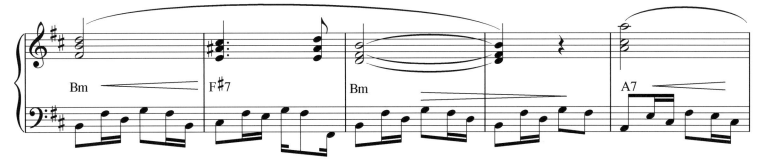

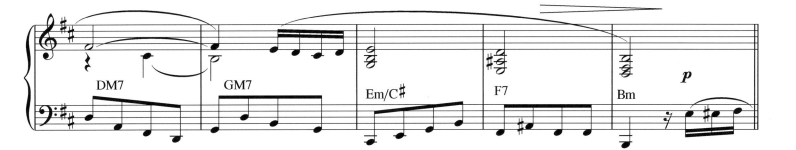

IRACUNDO

à la reprise, contrechant de violon, ou flûte, ou guit.

By ASTOR PIAZZOLLA

31

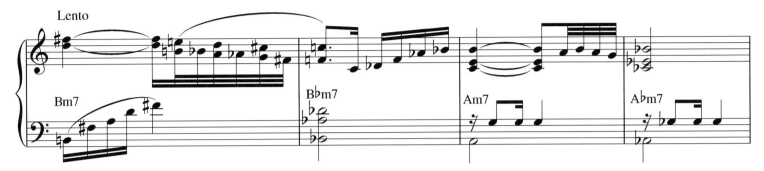

(Key change is for repeat only)

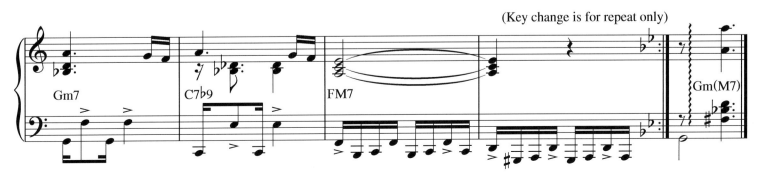

LA CALLE 92

Piano (Synthé) - Chant - Bandonéon (Accordéon) - Violon

By ASTOR PIAZZOLLA

Tango (respectez les nuances)

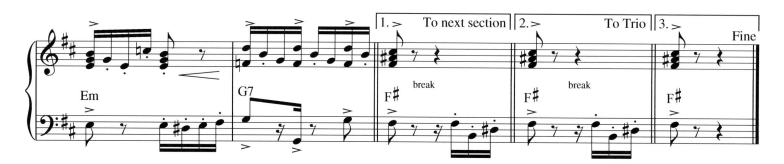

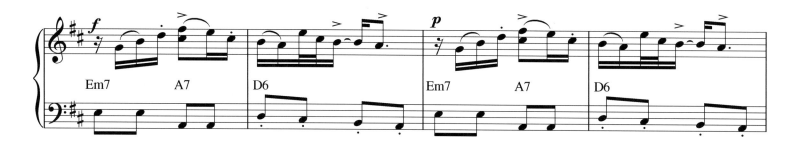

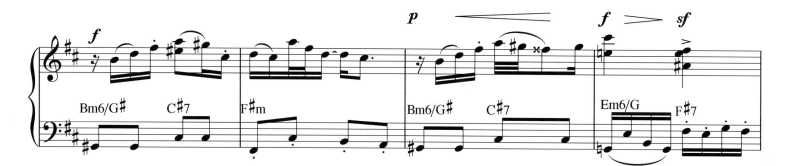

Trio
mf

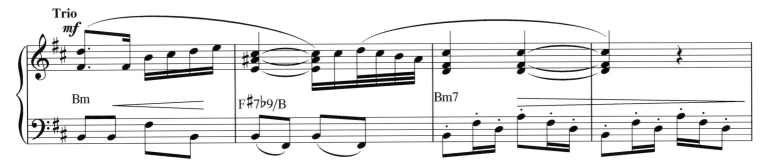

D.C.

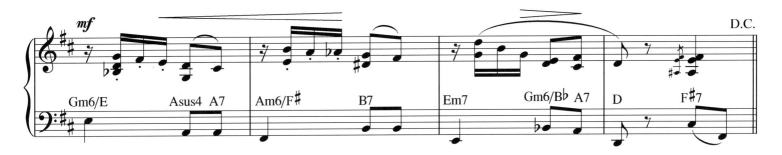

LA FIN DEL MUNDO

By OSCAR NICOLAS FRESEDO
and ASTOR PIAZZOLLA

35

luz de a-quel vie-jo fa-rol la vi-da te cam-bió, por o-tra de Mer-cu — rio.

Fm Fm7 G7 G7♭5 Cm7 G♭ B♭m

A mí no me cam-bia-ron tus lu-ces los a — ños.

B♭m E♭7 A♭ G7 B♭m7 E♭7

Hoy la gen-te sin pen-sar te de-ja, mi ar-ra-bal, so-ñan-do con as-fal — to

Fm Fm7 G7 G7♭5 Cm7 F7 B♭m

mu-chos pu-die-ron vo-lar se fué-ron de los gris, dé-ja-ron el per-cal...

E♭ E♭7 A♭ Fm7 B♭m7 E♭7 E♭m6 F7

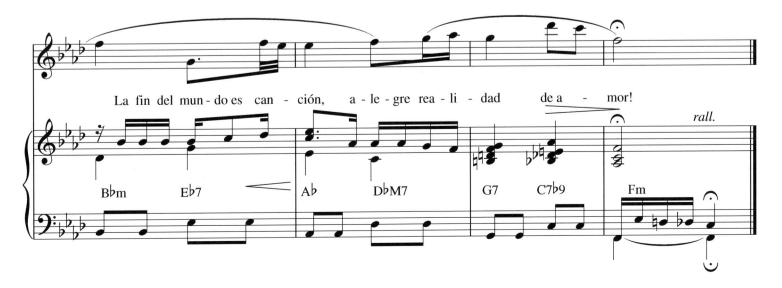

La fin del mun-do es can-ción, a-le-gre rea-li-dad de a-mor!

rall.

B♭m E♭7 A♭ D♭M7 G7 C7♭9 Fm

NUEVO MUNDO

By ASTOR PIAZZOLLA

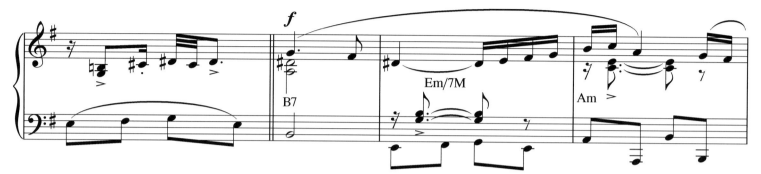

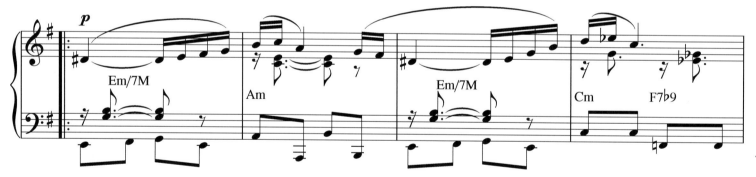

PRESENTANIA

By ROBERT AUGUSTE ENGEL
and ASTOR PIAZZOLLA

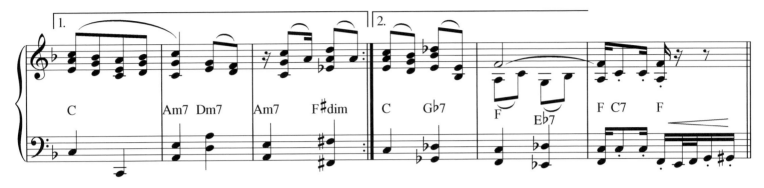

D.S. al Fine

PSICOSIS

PIANO - BANDONÉON (Accordéon) - VIOLON (Synthé) - BASSE

By ASTOR PIAZZOLLA

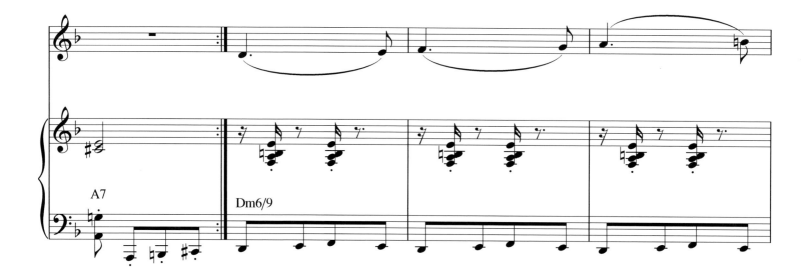

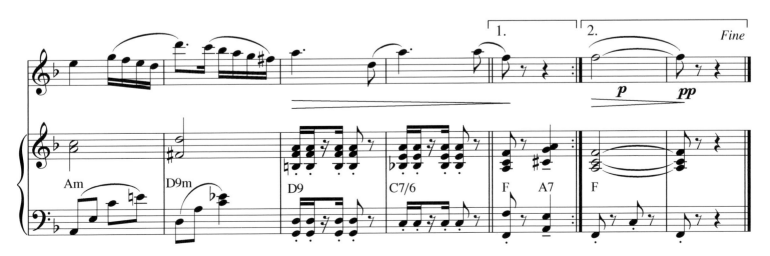

QUAND TU LIRAS CES MOTS
(Rosa Rio)

By JUAN CARLOS LA MADRID
and ASTOR PIAZZOLLA

- né
- né

De t'a voir trop ai - mé
Mais tu n'as rien gar - dé

Quand tu li -ras ce-
Quand tu li -ras ce-

Gm

Dm

- la
- la

sur - tout
A - lors

ne m'en veux pas.
tu com - pren -dras.

Fine

E7

A7

Dm

A7 Dm

Am7

Am6

F   A7

Dm

Dm/7M

mp

mp

f

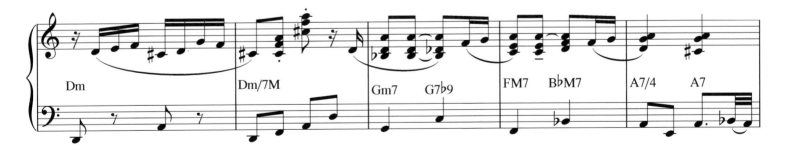

Dm

Dm/7M

Gm7   G7♭9

FM7   B♭M7

A7/4   A7

D.S. al Fine

Quand tu li-ras ces

Gm

B♭   A7

RECUERDO NEW YORK

By ASTOR PIAZZOLLA

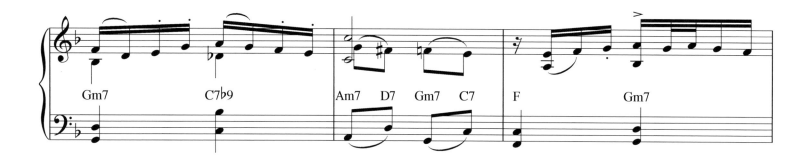

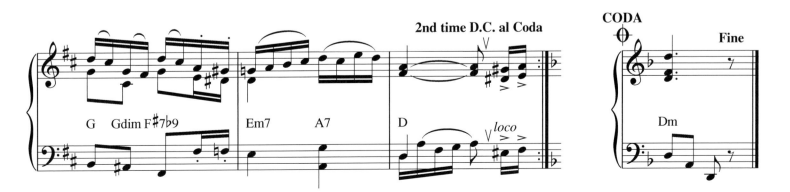

REVIRADO

By ASTOR PIAZZOLLA

Tango

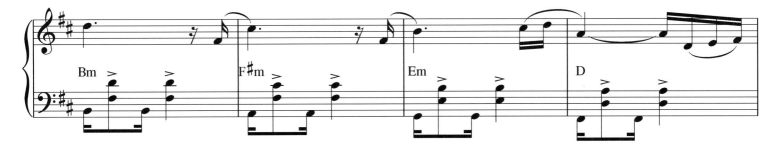

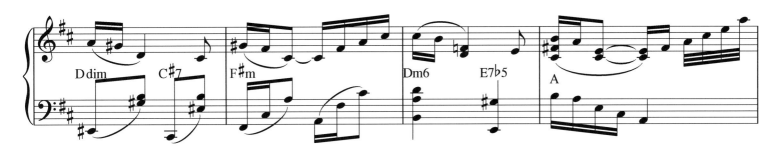

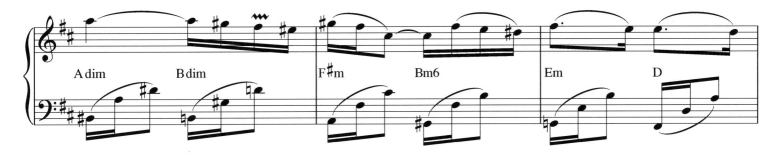

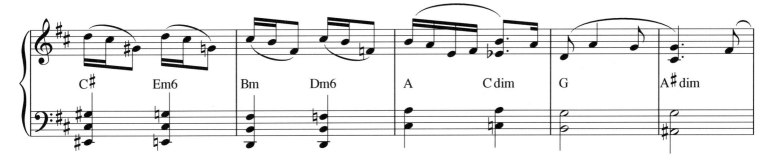

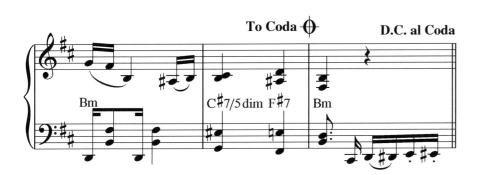

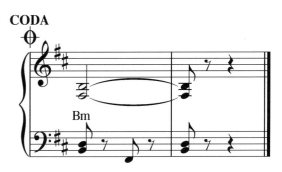

ROMANTICO IDILIO
(Sans ta présence)

By GUY FAVREAU, ALBERT ABRAHAM,
BEN SOUSSAN and ASTOR PIAZZOLLA

Tango

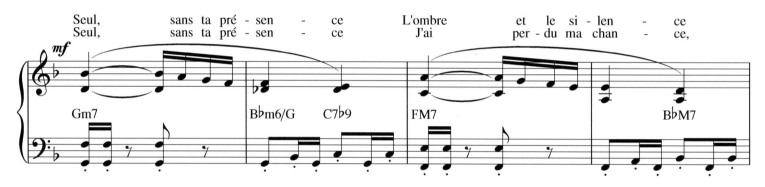

Seul, sans ta pré - sen - ce L'ombre et le si - len - ce
Seul, sans ta pré - sen - ce J'ai per - du ma chan - ce,

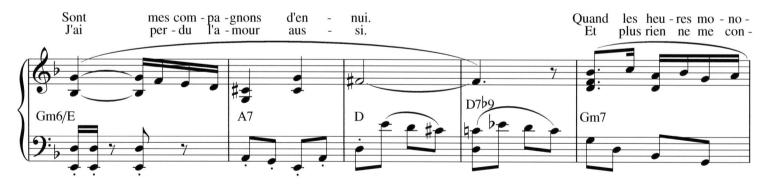

Sont mes com - pa - gnons d'en - nui. Quand les heu - res mo - no -
J'ai per - du l'a - mour aus - si. Et plus rien ne me con -

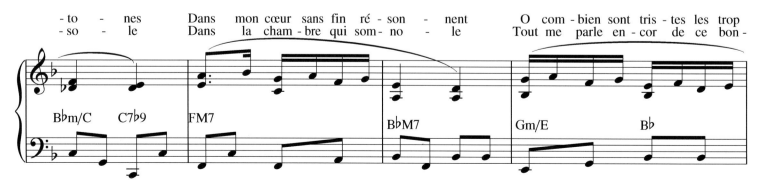

- to - nes Dans mon cœur sans fin ré - son - nent O com - bien sont tris - tes les trop
- so - le Dans la cham - bre qui som - no - le Tout me parle en - cor de ce bon -

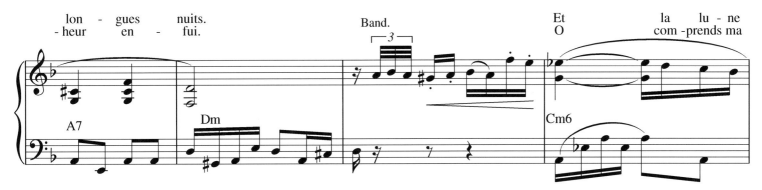

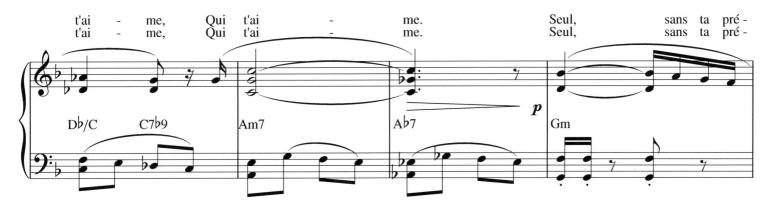

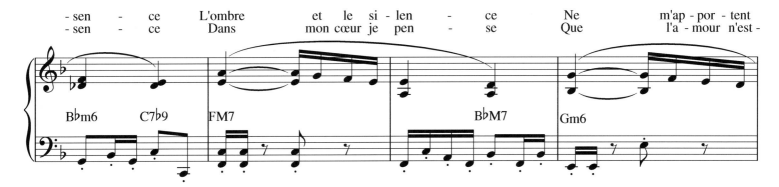

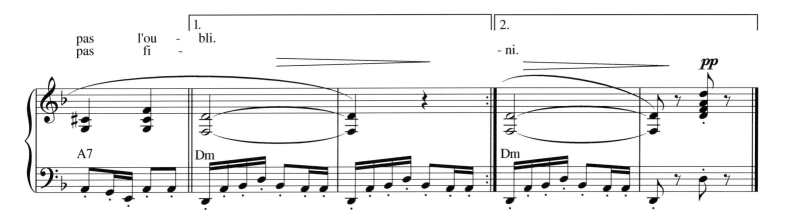

SE TERMINO
(C'est Fini)

By ASTOR PIAZZOLLA

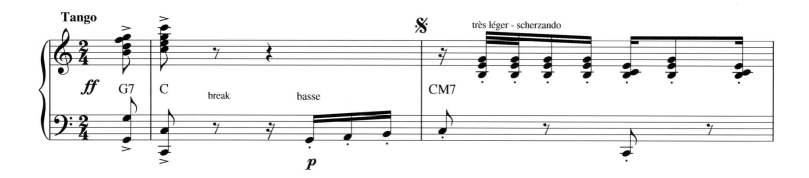

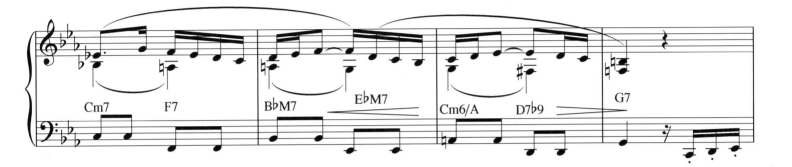

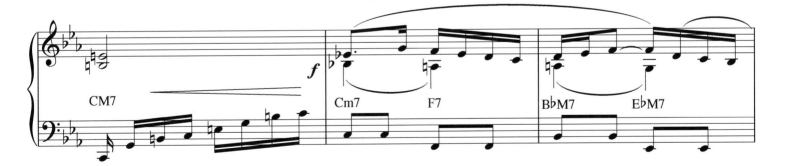

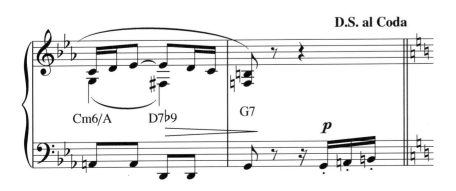

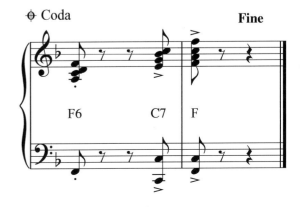

TANGO CHOC
(Doudou)

By ASTOR PIAZZOLLA

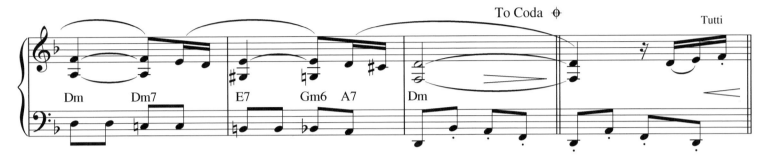

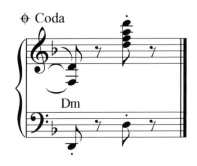

TANGUISIMO

PIANO - BANDONÉON (Accordéon) - VIOLON (Synthé) - BASSE

By ASTOR PIAZZOLLA

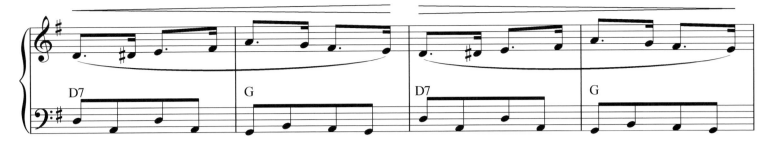

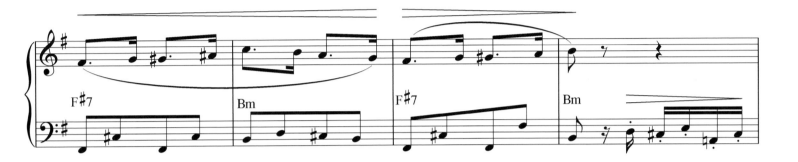

TE QUIERO TANGO

By ASTOR PIAZZOLLA

57

TODO FUÉ

By DIANA PIAZZOLLA
and ASTOR PIAZZOLLA

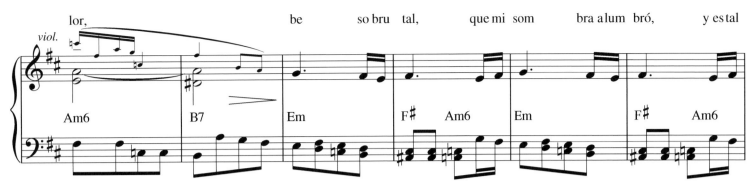

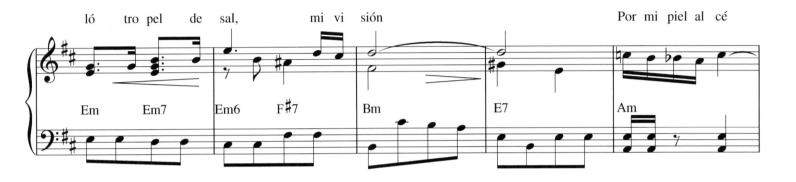

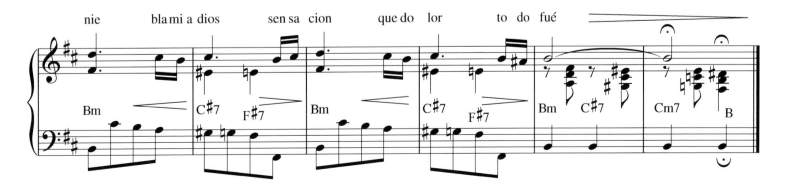

DÉTRESSE

Piano (Synthé) - Chant - Bandonéon (Accordéon) - Violon

By ASTOR PIAZZOLLA

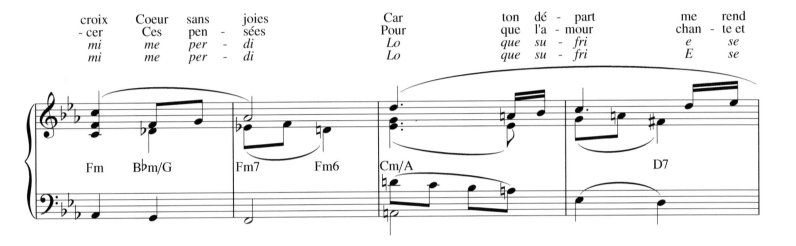

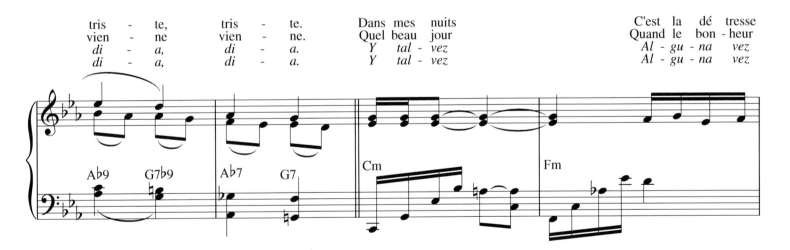

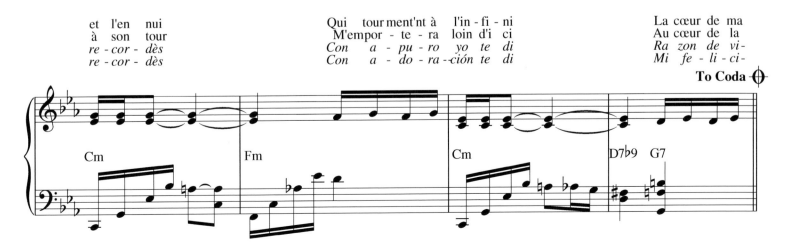

vie.

vir.

morendo

D.S. al Coda

CODA vie
- dad.

pppp

Fine

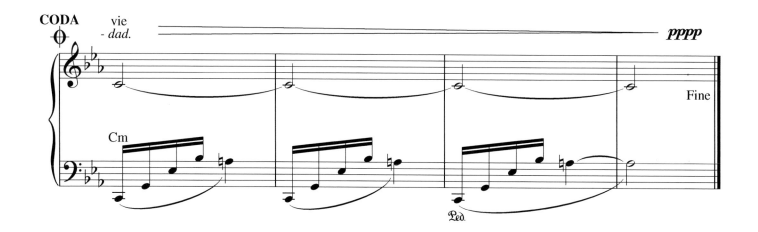